B.C. Great Zot, I'm Beautiful

Johnny Hart

CORONET BOOKS
Hodder Fawcett, London

Printed in Great Britain for Hodder Fawcett Ltd.,
Mill Road, Dunton Green, Sevenoaks, Kent
(Editorial Office: 47 Bedford Square,
London, WC1 3DP), by
Hunt Barnard Printing Ltd., Aylesbury, Bucks.

ISBN 0 340 21993 9

I'D LIKE ONE TICKET TO THE BEACH.
TICKETS
IS THAT THE OUTFIT YOU'RE WEARING?
YES.
6·18
SOLD OUT

6-22

CAN I APPLY FOR MEMBERSHIP IN YOUR SOCIETY?

THE INTELLECTUAL SOCIETY

REGISTRAR

6·28

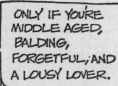

ONLY IF YOU'RE MIDDLE AGED, BALDING, FORGETFUL, AND A LOUSY LOVER.

I'M AFRAID I CAN'T QUALIFY ON THAT LAST ONE.

QUALIFY?.... YOU'RE IN CONTENTION FOR THE "GRAND SACHEM"!

hart

7.7

"RING"

NO, SHE'S NOT HERE RIGHT NOW, THIS IS HER GIRLFRIEND.

... WHAT DO I LOOK LIKE? ... WHY DON'T YOU COME OVER AND SEE, BIG BOY?

7·9

WHOOPS

ZIP

*SIGH...... ALMOST MADE IT TO THE CREST OF THE HILL.

7·10

WHAT CAN I DO TO BOOST SALES FOR MOUTHWASH?

WHAT YOU NEED IS A GIVE-AWAY PREMIUM ITEM.

PETER'S ADVERTISING AGENCY

7·17

THAT'S A GREAT IDEA.... WHAT DO YOU SUGGEST?

GARLIC FLAVORED TOOTHPASTE.

PETER'S ADVERTISING AGENCY

7.19

A NOTED PSYCHOLOGIST STATES THAT MAN'S INTELLIGENCE IS DIRECTLY PROPORTIONAL TO THE LENGTH OF HIS HAIR.

7·20

HI, STUPID.

WHAT BROUGHT THAT ON?

7-22

UH,.... WHAT'S THE "US" STAND FOR?

ME AND HIM.

ig·nite' *v.*

the evening of the annual IG festival.

WILEY'S DICTIONARY

WILEY'S DICTIONARY

7·24

7:26

7·27

THANKS FOR THE NEAT 'TAKE'.

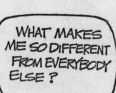

7·30

8·2

SLUURP

BE SURE TO TUNE IN TOMORROW FOR A MAMMOTH AARRGGHH.

AAAA RRGGHH

8·17

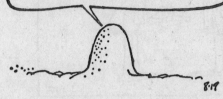

8-21

ZOT

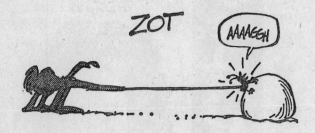

8-27

9-2

94

9·10

9.11

WHAT CAN YOU GIVE ME TO CURE MY INSOMNIA?

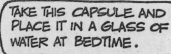

TAKE THIS CAPSULE AND PLACE IT IN A GLASS OF WATER AT BEDTIME.

PETER'S PHARMACY

9.15

WHAT DOES THAT DO?

IT TURNS IT INTO A BOOK ENTITLED: "1001 WAYS TO EMBALM A BUTTERFLY.

PETER'S PHARMACY

merit

WHAT KIND OF PILLS DO YOU HAVE TO PREVENT FALLING ASLEEP ON THE WHEEL?

PETER'S PHARMACY

9·16

TRY THESE "NOSNOOZ". TAKE ONE EVERY THREE MILES TILL YOU REACH YOUR DESTINATION.

PETER'S PHARMACY

Dear nosnooze,
I have a problem,...
It has been 2 years
now since I completed
my round the world
excursion ....

9·22

9.27

9-29

THERE MUST BE SOME REASON WHY WE'RE HERE.

OF COURSE THERE IS, STUPID! ...

10·4

WE'RE HERE TO PROLIFERATE THE SPECIES!

LET'S LEAVE THE I.R.S. OUT OF THIS! .·..WHY ARE WE **REALLY** HERE?

108

HEY, THESE PRICES ARE REALLY REASONABLE! HOW DO YOU DO IT?

NO OVERHEAD.

SLITHER
SLITHER
KA-PUNK

SLITHER
KA-PUNK
SLITHER

KA-PUNK
SLITHER
KA-PUNK

WHAT CAN
I DO FOR
YOU FRIEND?

THOR'S
SERVICE
STATION

10·18

I THINK I BLEW
ONE OF MY
HORNY
PLATES.

THOR'S
SERVICE
STATION

10·19

10·20

10·22

10-30

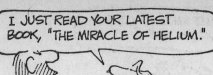

11·2

11.3

11·5

11-8

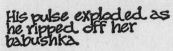

8

YOU'RE LATEST BOOK LOOKS GREAT!

HOW DO YOU WRITERS COME UP WITH THOSE FANTASTIC IDEAS?

PETER'S PUBLISHING CO.

11·11

LIKE, I MEAN, WHO WOULD EVER THINK OF PUTTING A LAME-BRAINED IDIOT IN CHARGE OF A PUBLISHING COMPAN......

11·15

YOU LEFT OUT THE "B".

ZANG

"..LIKE MY NIFTY MURAL?..."

11-22

SOME OF THE OTHER GREAT B.C. TITLES
AVAILABLE IN CORONET BOOKS

All these books are available at your local bookshop or newsagent, or can be ordered direct from the publisher. Just tick the titles you want and fill in the form below.

Prices and availability subject to change without notice.

CORONET BOOKS, P.O. Box 11, Falmouth, Cornwall.

Please send cheque or postal order, and allow the following for postage and packing:

U.K. – One book 22p plus 10p per copy for each additional book ordered, up to a maximum of 82p.

B.F.P.O. and EIRE – 22p for the first book plus 10p per copy for the next 6 books, thereafter 4p per book.

OTHER OVERSEAS CUSTOMERS – 30p for the first book and 10p per copy for each additional book.

Name ....

Address ....

....